CULTURES OF THE WORLD! SOUTH AFRICA, NIGERIA & EGYPT
CULTURE FOR KIDS
CHILDREN'S CULTURAL STUDIES BOOKS

All Rights reserved. No part of this book may be reproduced or used in any way or form or by any means whether electronic or mechanical, this means that you cannot record or photocopy any material ideas or tips that are provided in this book

Copyright 2016

In this book, you will learn the cultures of South Africa, Nigeria and Egypt. Learning other people's culture can help us become more appreciative of others.

SOUTH AFRICA

It is called the Rainbow Nation. The phrase describes the country's multicultural diversity. Around 80% of the population is composed of black South Africans. They belong to a variety of ethnic groups.

A large number of white South Africans of Afrikaans and English background is a result of the country's colonial past. The prominent influences are Christianity, Islam, Indian, and traditional African cultures.

Black African culture is best known for its art, dance and music. More than two centuries of colonialism and the work of Christian missionaries have deeply influenced their art, dance and music.

South African visual art is a combination of traditional and modern. Artists are greatly inspired by statues, figurines, and masks of tribal cultures. Western techniques and mediums are also employed in their works.

The beaded jewelry tradition in South Africa is dependent on European beads. The beads were brought as barter for African goods. Large and tiny glass beads were exchanged by European traders.

There are many different ethnic groups in South Africa aside from the native South Africans. There are 9 officially-recognized local languages. South African tribal cultures are rich in oral traditions. Their stories, epics and poems were recited out loud. These stories and poems have greatly influenced written literature.

NIGERIA

Nigeria has 521 languages. English is the official language of Nigeria. It is to facilitate the cultural and linguistic unity of the country, after it was colonized by the British. It is also widely used in education, and for official purposes and business transactions.

The Nigerians follow many religions because the constitution grants them freedom of religion. The Christians occupy the southern part of the country, while the Muslims live in the north. Native religions are also followed throughout the country.

Generally, Nigerians are proud of their country. Nigeria is also a super-power in the African continent along with South Africa. It is endowed with vast quantities of natural resources. Nigeria is the sixth largest oil-producing nation. Its society is well-educated and industrious.

The extended family is the backbone of the social system. All family members work as a unit throughout their lives. They help one another. Family members are expected to help and extend support for the welfare of every member.

People are addressed by their surname and their professional and academic titles. Bowing one's head is necessary in greeting someone who is older. It is a sign of respect.

Nigerians are outgoing and friendly. Their communication style is generally polite, although Nigerians' styles of communication vary. Nigerians in the south are more direct in their speech. Their voice tends to be louder. They raise their voices if they are excited.

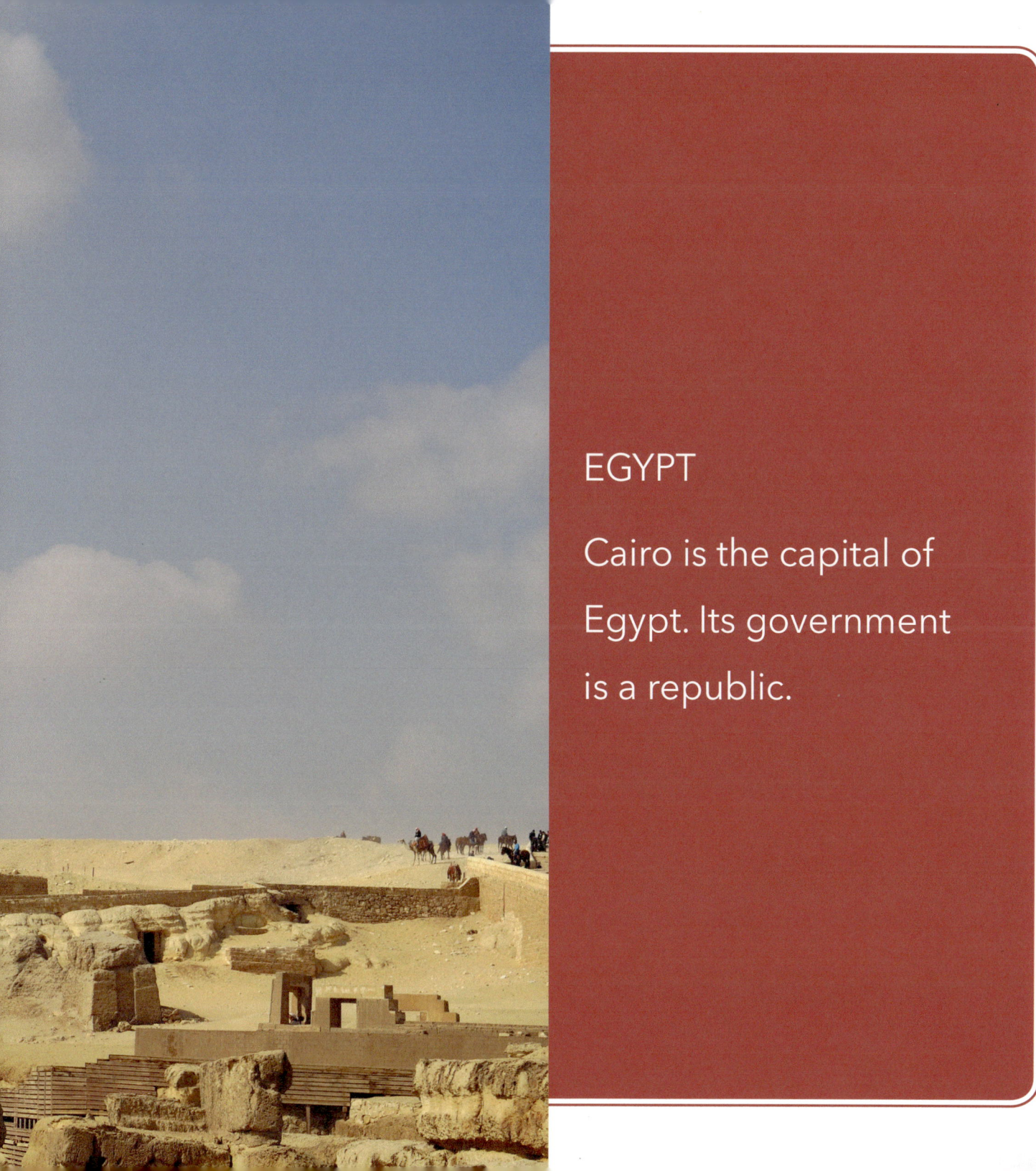

EGYPT

Cairo is the capital of Egypt. Its government is a republic.

Egyptian culture can be traced back to the times of the ancient Pharaohs. Foreign visitors might observe that Egyptians are mild-mannered and very polite people. It is the result of their religious principles. One should have a broad understanding of the Egyptian culture to have a successful visit to this country.

Arabic has been the written and spoken language for almost 13 centuries, since the arrival of Islam and Arabic culture from the Arabian peninsula.

The majority of Egyptians practice Islam. This religion emanated from Saudi Arabia. They observe the practices of all other Muslims in the world. These include fasting during Ramadan, praying five times a day, taking a pilgrimage to Mecca, and many others.

An important facet of interpersonal relationships is honor. Part of this is to be hospitable to friends and guests. People should respect their elders and those in authority. A man should stand by his words.

Learning the cultures of countries will give us a clue on how their people act and interact. It will help us to understand and appreciate them more. Researching culture, manners and etiquette will help us to deal with people better.

Made in United States
Troutdale, OR
11/24/2023